MAD LIBS®

KEEP THE FAITH MAD LIBS

by Heather

MAD LIBS

An imprint of Penguin Random House LLC, New York

First published in the United States of America by Mad Libs,
an imprint of Penguin Random House LLC, New York, 2023

Mad Libs format and text copyright © 2023 by Penguin Random House LLC

Concept created by Roger Price & Leonard Stern

Cover illustration by Scott Brooks

Visit us online at penguinrandomhouse.com.

Printed in the United States of America

ISBN 9780593658604
1 3 5 7 9 10 8 6 4 2
COMR

MAD LIBS

INSTRUCTIONS

MAD LIBS® is a game for people who don't like games!
It can be played by one, two, three, four, or forty.

• RIDICULOUSLY SIMPLE DIRECTIONS

In this tablet you will find stories containing blank spaces where words
are left out. One player, the READER, selects one of these stories. The
READER does not tell anyone what the story is about. Instead, he/she asks
the other players, the WRITERS, to give him/her words. These words are
used to fill in the blank spaces in the story.

• TO PLAY

The READER asks each WRITER in turn to call out a word—an adjective or
a noun or whatever the space calls for—and uses them to fill in the blank
spaces in the story. The result is a MAD LIBS® game.

When the READER then reads the completed MAD LIBS® game to the other
players, they will discover that they have written a story that is fantastic,
screamingly funny, shocking, silly, crazy, or just plain dumb—depending
upon which words each WRITER called out.

• EXAMPLE (*Before* and *After*)

"_____!" he said _____
  EXCLAMATION   ADVERB

as he jumped into his convertible _____ and
                                        NOUN

drove off with his _____ wife.
                        ADJECTIVE

"____OUCH____!" he said ____HAPPILY____
  EXCLAMATION   ADVERB

as he jumped into his convertible ____CAT____ and
                                        NOUN

drove off with his ____BRAVE____ wife.
                        ADJECTIVE

MAD LIBS

QUICK REVIEW

In case you have forgotten what adjectives, adverbs, nouns, and verbs are, here is a quick review:

An ADJECTIVE describes something or somebody. *Lumpy*, *soft*, *ugly*, *messy*, and *short* are adjectives.

An ADVERB tells how something is done. It modifies a verb and usually ends in "ly." *Modestly*, *stupidly*, *greedily*, and *carefully* are adverbs.

A NOUN is the name of a person, place, or thing. *Sidewalk*, *umbrella*, *bridle*, *bathtub*, and *nose* are nouns.

A VERB is an action word. *Run*, *pitch*, *jump*, and *swim* are verbs. Put the verbs in past tense if the directions say PAST TENSE. *Ran*, *pitched*, *jumped*, and *swam* are verbs in the past tense.

When we ask for A PLACE, we mean any sort of place: a country or city (*Spain*, *Cleveland*) or a room (*bathroom*, *kitchen*).

An EXCLAMATION or SILLY WORD is any sort of funny sound, gasp, grunt, or outcry, like *Wow!*, *Ouch!*, *Whomp!*, *Ick!*, and *Gadzooks!*

When we ask for specific words, like a NUMBER, a COLOR, an ANIMAL, or a PART OF THE BODY, we mean a word that is one of those things, like *seven*, *blue*, *horse*, or *head*.

When we ask for a PLURAL, it means more than one. For example, *cat* pluralized is *cats*.

MAD LIBS® is fun to play with friends, but you can also play it by yourself! To begin with, DO NOT look at the story on the page below. Fill in the blanks on this page with the words called for. Then, using the words you have selected, fill in the blank spaces in the story.

Now you've created your own hilarious MAD LIBS® game!

THE UNWRITTEN RULES OF YOUTH GROUP FIELD TRIPS

NUMBER _____

PLURAL NOUN _____

ADJECTIVE _____

PERSON YOU KNOW _____

VEHICLE _____

COLOR _____

TYPE OF LIQUID _____

CELEBRITY _____

CELEBRITY _____

PART OF THE BODY _____

ADVERB _____

PLURAL NOUN _____

PERSON FROM HISTORY _____

A PLACE _____

TYPE OF FOOD _____

ADJECTIVE _____

SOMETHING ALIVE (PLURAL) _____

MAD LIBS®
THE UNWRITTEN RULES OF YOUTH GROUP FIELD TRIPS

Here are the rules of youth group field trips:

- There are _____ vans, and one of them always smells like
  <u>NUMBER</u>

  stinky _____. Arrive early to get on the non-
  <u>PLURAL NOUN</u>

  _____ van.
  <u>ADJECTIVE</u>

- Let _____ sit in the front seat because they get
  <u>PERSON YOU KNOW</u>

  _____ sick. If they sit in the back, they throw up
  <u>VEHICLE</u>

  _____ _____.
  <u>COLOR</u>   <u>TYPE OF LIQUID</u>

- Pastor _____ will blare worship songs by _____,
  <u>CELEBRITY</u>   <u>CELEBRITY</u>

  so come prepared with _____-buds.
  <u>PART OF THE BODY</u>

- Every time the driver turns the bus _____, smoosh the
  <u>ADVERB</u>

  _____ sitting by the windows.
  <u>PLURAL NOUN</u>

- Never look bored, or adult leaders will ask about your relationship

  with _____.
  <u>PERSON FROM HISTORY</u>

- Whether you're headed for a relaxing day at (the) _____ or
  <u>A PLACE</u>

  to give _____ to the hungry, remember to have _____
  <u>TYPE OF FOOD</u>   <u>ADJECTIVE</u>

  fun and love all of God's _____.
  <u>SOMETHING ALIVE (PLURAL)</u>

MAD LIBS® is fun to play with friends, but you can also play it by yourself! To begin with, DO NOT look at the story on the page below. Fill in the blanks on this page with the words called for. Then, using the words you have selected, fill in the blank spaces in the story.

Now you've created your own hilarious MAD LIBS® game!

WINTER YOUTH RETREAT

NOUN _____

NOUN _____

TYPE OF EVENT _____

SILLY WORD _____

VERB _____

NOUN _____

A PLACE _____

ARTICLE OF CLOTHING (PLURAL) _____

NOUN _____

SOMETHING ALIVE (PLURAL) _____

NOUN _____

NOUN _____

ADJECTIVE _____

NOUN _____

VERB _____

NOUN _____

VERB ENDING IN "ING" _____

NOUN _____

MAD LIBS®

WINTER YOUTH RETREAT

Presidents' _____ weekend is just around the _____!
                 NOUN   NOUN

Don't miss our Winter Youth _____, where you can:
                            TYPE OF EVENT

- Explore God's creation in the beautiful _____ Mountains!
                                          SILLY WORD

- Slip and _____ your way to victory in a/an _____
            VERB   NOUN

  hockey tournament!

- Hike through a beautiful evergreen _____
                                          A PLACE

  in snow- _____!
           ARTICLE OF CLOTHING (PLURAL)

- Enjoy really fun snow- _____ fights with your best
                              NOUN

  _____!
  SOMETHING ALIVE (PLURAL)

- Race down a snowy _____ in a bobsled made of
                         NOUN

  _____-board!
    NOUN

- Dance to _____ music with a live _____!
            ADJECTIVE   NOUN

- _____ new friendships and read the Bible next to a roaring
  VERB

  _____!
    NOUN

What are you _____ for? Grab a knit _____ to
             VERB ENDING IN "ING"   NOUN

wear on your head and sign up now!

MAD LIBS® is fun to play with friends, but you can also play it by yourself! To begin with, DO NOT look at the story on the page below. Fill in the blanks on this page with the words called for. Then, using the words you have selected, fill in the blank spaces in the story.

Now you've created your own hilarious MAD LIBS® game!

FUNDRAISING FEBRUARY

PLURAL NOUN _____

TYPE OF FOOD _____

TYPE OF FOOD (PLURAL) _____

TYPE OF CONTAINER _____

FIRST NAME _____

NUMBER _____

COLOR _____

PLURAL NOUN _____

SOMETHING ALIVE (PLURAL) _____

TYPE OF EVENT _____

PLURAL NOUN _____

NUMBER _____

NUMBER _____

TYPE OF EVENT _____

VERB _____

PLURAL NOUN _____

VERB _____

TYPE OF BUILDING _____

MAD LIBS®

FUNDRAISING FEBRUARY

It's time for Fundraising February, the month that our church sets aside

to raise _____ for charities. The first Sunday, the teens will
     PLURAL NOUN

host a bake sale, selling homemade _____ brownies, oatmeal
                             TYPE OF FOOD

raisin _____, and red velvet _____-cakes.
    TYPE OF FOOD (PLURAL)   TYPE OF CONTAINER

The second weekend, the adults will host a/an _____ Bond–
                                     FIRST NAME

themed casino night, where those over the age of _____ can play
                                   NUMBER

_____-jack or drop their quarters in slot _____.
  COLOR   PLURAL NOUN

Invite the _____ in your neighborhood. The
       SOMETHING ALIVE (PLURAL)

third weekend, we'll host a silent _____, and we'll be
                           TYPE OF EVENT

auctioning off artistic _____, _____-day trips to
               PLURAL NOUN   NUMBER

New York City, and even a/an _____-dollar gift card to the
                        NUMBER

famous _____ in France. The final weekend, we will be
    TYPE OF EVENT

doing a/an _____-a-thon, where the little kids will raise
         VERB

_____ for every mile they _____ around the
  PLURAL NOUN   VERB

_____.
TYPE OF BUILDING

MAD LIBS® is fun to play with friends, but you can also play it by yourself! To begin with, DO NOT look at the story on the page below. Fill in the blanks on this page with the words called for. Then, using the words you have selected, fill in the blank spaces in the story.

Now you've created your own hilarious MAD LIBS® game!

LENT

SOMETHING ALIVE (PLURAL) _____

TYPE OF LIQUID _____

ADJECTIVE _____

EXCLAMATION _____

COLOR _____

VERB ENDING IN "ING" _____

VERB _____

VERB ENDING IN "ING" _____

PLURAL NOUN _____

ADJECTIVE _____

PART OF THE BODY _____

VERB ENDING IN "ING" _____

SILLY WORD _____

NUMBER _____

SAME SILLY WORD _____

PLURAL NOUN _____

VERB _____

MAD LIBS®

LENT

Two _____ are talking about Lent, the
SOMETHING ALIVE (PLURAL)

forty days when Christians give up something to prepare their hearts

for Jesus's death and resurrection:

Kid 1: I'm giving up _____ and _____ candy.
TYPE OF LIQUID   ADJECTIVE

Kid 2: _____! I'm giving up _____ vegetables.
EXCLAMATION   COLOR

Kid 1: That's _____! You have to _____ up
VERB ENDING IN "ING"   VERB

something you love, like _____ video _____.
VERB ENDING IN "ING"   PLURAL NOUN

Lent helps us remember how God sacrificed for us. You could also

break a/an _____ habit, like biting your _____ or
ADJECTIVE   PART OF THE BODY

_____ your knuckles.
VERB ENDING IN "ING"

Kid 2: I say _____ at least _____ times a day.
SILLY WORD   NUMBER

Kid 1: Perfect! Instead of saying _____, you can pray and
SAME SILLY WORD

thank God for all your _____!
PLURAL NOUN

Kid 2: Okay! As long as I don't have to _____ vegetables, I
VERB

love Lent!

MAD LIBS® is fun to play with friends, but you can also play it by yourself! To begin with, DO NOT look at the story on the page below. Fill in the blanks on this page with the words called for. Then, using the words you have selected, fill in the blank spaces in the story.

Now you've created your own hilarious MAD LIBS® game!

IT'S PALM SUNDAY

NUMBER _____

ADJECTIVE _____

VERB _____

PART OF THE BODY _____

EXCLAMATION _____

YOUR NAME _____

NOUN _____

NOUN _____

PART OF THE BODY (PLURAL) _____

VERB ENDING IN "ING" _____

ARTICLE OF CLOTHING (PLURAL) _____

NOUN _____

NOUN _____

SOMETHING ALIVE (PLURAL) _____

TYPE OF BUILDING _____

MAD LIBS®

IT'S PALM SUNDAY

Today at church, I was given _____ very long and _____
                              NUMBER   ADJECTIVE

palm leaves called fronds. I learned you shouldn't _____ your
                                                        VERB

sister on the _____ with them when my sister yelled,
              PART OF THE BODY

" _____," and my mom whispered, "Stop it, _____,
   EXCLAMATION   YOUR NAME

or you'll be in for a big _____." I also learned to not twist the
                         NOUN

fronds into the shape of a/an _____. Dad glared at me with
                              NOUN

his _____ when I did that. Instead, he showed me
    PART OF THE BODY (PLURAL)

how to make a cross out of the palm fronds by _____
                                              VERB ENDING IN "ING"

the fronds in a simple knot. Tying the knot was as easy as tying my

shoe- _____! After church, we're supposed to
      ARTICLE OF CLOTHING (PLURAL)

put the cross where we will see it, like on the bedside _____
                                                       NOUN

or the bathroom _____. The palm-frond cross helps us
                NOUN

remember Jesus's triumphal entry into Jerusalem. I put mine on my

dresser next to my favorite stuffed _____
                                    SOMETHING ALIVE (PLURAL)

and my doll- _____. I knew if I kept the cross there, I'd
             TYPE OF BUILDING

never forget how much Jesus loves me!

MAD LIBS® is fun to play with friends, but you can also play it by yourself! To begin with, DO NOT look at the story on the page below. Fill in the blanks on this page with the words called for. Then, using the words you have selected, fill in the blank spaces in the story.

Now you've created your own hilarious MAD LIBS® game!

MY EASTER POEM

PLURAL NOUN _____

TYPE OF FOOD (PLURAL) _____

VERB (PAST TENSE) _____

ADJECTIVE _____

ANIMAL _____

ADJECTIVE _____

ADVERB _____

VERB ENDING IN "S" _____

PLURAL NOUN _____

TYPE OF CONTAINER (PLURAL) _____

PLURAL NOUN _____

COLOR _____

ANIMAL (PLURAL) _____

ADJECTIVE _____

TYPE OF EVENT _____

VERB _____

MAD LIBS®

MY EASTER POEM

No matter what other _____ say,
PLURAL NOUN

Easter is the best holiday.

I love dipping Easter _____ in dye
TYPE OF FOOD (PLURAL)

and getting _____ on Sunday in my _____ bow tie!
VERB (PAST TENSE)   ADJECTIVE

I love the Easter _____ and its cute, _____ nose,
ANIMAL   ADJECTIVE

who _____ _____ lots of colorful
ADVERB   VERB ENDING IN "S"

_____ everywhere it goes.
PLURAL NOUN

I love Easter _____ and _____,
TYPE OF CONTAINER (PLURAL)   PLURAL NOUN

all _____ and yellow
COLOR

and filled with baby _____ made of marshmallow.
ANIMAL (PLURAL)

But the _____ thing about this _____
ADJECTIVE   TYPE OF EVENT

isn't something we _____,
VERB

it's just knowing in my heart that God loves me and you.

MAD LIBS® is fun to play with friends, but you can also play it by yourself! To begin with, DO NOT look at the story on the page below. Fill in the blanks on this page with the words called for. Then, using the words you have selected, fill in the blank spaces in the story.

Now you've created your own hilarious MAD LIBS® game!

CHURCH BARBECUE

NOUN _____

PART OF THE BODY (PLURAL) _____

VERB _____

PERSON YOU KNOW _____

TYPE OF FOOD _____

PERSON YOU KNOW _____

TYPE OF LIQUID _____

TYPE OF FOOD _____

ADJECTIVE _____

PLURAL NOUN _____

ANIMAL (PLURAL) _____

PART OF THE BODY (PLURAL) _____

PLURAL NOUN _____

VERB _____

ANIMAL _____

VERB _____

PLURAL NOUN _____

ANIMAL _____

MAD LIBS®

CHURCH BARBECUE

In June, when the weather's good and the _____ is shining, we have
                                         NOUN

a barbecue after church! After we bow our _____
                                           PART OF THE BODY (PLURAL)

and give thanks for the food, it's time to _____!
                                            VERB

_____ cooks the best hamburgers. I like my burger with
PERSON YOU KNOW

melted _____ on top. _____ brings the chili. It's so
        TYPE OF FOOD   PERSON YOU KNOW

spicy, I always have to drink lots of _____. Mayra usually
                                       TYPE OF LIQUID

brings dessert, but last time she accidentally used salt instead of sugar

in the chocolate chip _____, which tasted _____.
                       TYPE OF FOOD   ADJECTIVE

This Sunday, they asked her instead to bring plates, cups, and

_____. Brian loves to bring his specialty: _____
PLURAL NOUN   ANIMAL (PLURAL)

in a blanket. It's my favorite dish, _____ down.
                                      PART OF THE BODY (PLURAL)

While the adults sit at picnic _____ and chat, the kids
                               PLURAL NOUN

_____ on the playground, swing on the _____ bars,
VERB   ANIMAL

or play hide-and-go- _____. If I play my _____
                      VERB   PLURAL NOUN

right and stay to help clean up, I can take some leftovers home to feed

my _____.
    ANIMAL

MAD LIBS® is fun to play with friends, but you can also play it by yourself! To begin with, DO NOT look at the story on the page below. Fill in the blanks on this page with the words called for. Then, using the words you have selected, fill in the blank spaces in the story.

Now you've created your own hilarious MAD LIBS® game!

CHURCH BULLETIN ANNOUNCEMENT

EXCLAMATION _____

VERB _____

ADVERB _____

NOUN _____

OCCUPATION (PLURAL) _____

ADJECTIVE _____

NUMBER _____

NOUN _____

PERSON YOU KNOW _____

COLOR _____

ARTICLE OF CLOTHING _____

SOMETHING ALIVE (PLURAL) _____

CELEBRITY _____

ADJECTIVE _____

VEHICLE _____

TYPE OF BUILDING _____

PLURAL NOUN _____

MAD LIBS®
CHURCH BULLETIN ANNOUNCEMENT

See You at the Pole

_____! It's time for _____ You at the Pole, the
  EXCLAMATION   VERB

global day of student prayer!

Who: You! Invite your friends! The gathering is _____
                                                        ADVERB

_____-led with no parents or _____ allowed.
  NOUN   OCCUPATION (PLURAL)

When: Arrive _____ and early, at _____ o'clock on the
                ADJECTIVE   NUMBER

fourth Wednesday in September.

Where: The school flagpole in front of the _____ courts.
                                             NOUN

Look for _____. They will be wearing a/an _____
     PERSON YOU KNOW   COLOR

_____ that reads "Pray for _____!"
ARTICLE OF CLOTHING   SOMETHING ALIVE (PLURAL)

Coach _____ will attach _____ balloons to their
     CELEBRITY   ADJECTIVE

_____ and park it at the _____ .
  VEHICLE   TYPE OF BUILDING

Can't wait to see you all there as we pray for our schools, churches,

friends, and _____!
     PLURAL NOUN

MAD LIBS® is fun to play with friends, but you can also play it by yourself! To begin with, DO NOT look at the story on the page below. Fill in the blanks on this page with the words called for. Then, using the words you have selected, fill in the blank spaces in the story.

Now you've created your own hilarious MAD LIBS® game!

FALL LOCK-IN SCHEDULE

TYPE OF FOOD _____

TYPE OF LIQUID _____

PART OF THE BODY (PLURAL) _____

SOMETHING ALIVE _____

YOUR NAME _____

VERB _____

VERB ENDING IN "ING" _____

CELEBRITY _____

OCCUPATION _____

VERB _____

PERSON YOU KNOW _____

ADJECTIVE _____

NUMBER _____

PLURAL NOUN _____

NOUN _____

TYPE OF BUILDING _____

ADJECTIVE _____

MAD LIBS
FALL LOCK-IN SCHEDULE

Fall Lock-In Schedule!

Can't wait for the church all-nighter!

6:00: Dinner. Why do leaders always order Canadian bacon and

_____ pizza?
<small>TYPE OF FOOD</small>

7:00: _____-breakers like elbow tag and linking
<small>TYPE OF LIQUID</small>

_____ with a sweaty _____.
<small>PART OF THE BODY (PLURAL)</small>   <small>SOMETHING ALIVE</small>

8:00: Games. In mafia, if _____ is the doctor, they only
<small>YOUR NAME</small>

save themselves! _____-ball is my favorite, but I'm not great
<small>VERB</small>

at _____ balls flying at me.
<small>VERB ENDING IN "ING"</small>

9:00: Worship. Our leader _____ is good at playing guitar
<small>CELEBRITY</small>

even though they're a/an _____.
<small>OCCUPATION</small>

10:30: Leader hide-and-go- _____. Remember when
<small>VERB</small>

_____ got stuck in the _____ cabinet last year?
<small>PERSON YOU KNOW</small>   <small>ADJECTIVE</small>

12:00: Midnight movie. *13 Going on _____* or *Honey I Shrunk*
<small>NUMBER</small>

the _____.
<small>PLURAL NOUN</small>

2:00: *Mario* _____ tourney in the _____.
<small>NOUN</small>   <small>TYPE OF BUILDING</small>

6:00: Home. Sleep in my _____ bed!
<small>ADJECTIVE</small>

MAD LIBS® is fun to play with friends, but you can also play it by yourself! To begin with, DO NOT look at the story on the page below. Fill in the blanks on this page with the words called for. Then, using the words you have selected, fill in the blank spaces in the story.

Now you've created your own hilarious MAD LIBS® game!

LATE FOR CHURCH

EXCLAMATION _____

NUMBER _____

ADJECTIVE _____

PART OF THE BODY (PLURAL) _____

A SOUND _____

YOUR NAME _____

VERB _____

ADVERB _____

ARTICLE OF CLOTHING _____

ARTICLE OF CLOTHING (PLURAL) _____

VERB _____

NOUN _____

PART OF THE BODY (PLURAL) _____

PART OF THE BODY (PLURAL) _____

TYPE OF FOOD _____

NOUN _____

NOUN _____

SAME NOUN _____

LATE FOR CHURCH

_____! I'm late for church! I must have accidentally set my
EXCLAMATION

alarm for _____ o'clock in the evening instead of the morning.
NUMBER

Mom stomps into my _____ bedroom, puts her
ADJECTIVE

_____ on her hips, and lets out an angry _____.
PART OF THE BODY (PLURAL) A SOUND

She yells, "_____! Let's go!" I _____ out of bed
YOUR NAME VERB

and _____ throw on my best knitted _____
ADVERB ARTICLE OF CLOTHING

and freshly ironed _____. My sister is still in
ARTICLE OF CLOTHING (PLURAL)

the bathroom, so I _____ loudly on the door. She exits
VERB

and I race to the sink, turn on the _____, and brush my
NOUN

_____. I use a hairbrush to untangle my
PART OF THE BODY (PLURAL)

_____ and head to the kitchen to eat some scrambled
PART OF THE BODY (PLURAL)

_____. Dad's already waiting in the car with my sister and
TYPE OF FOOD

mom, and he honks the _____. I grab my _____ off
NOUN NOUN

the bookshelf—I never go to church without it—and then skip out the

door with my _____ in hand!
SAME NOUN

MAD LIBS® is fun to play with friends, but you can also play it by yourself! To begin with, DO NOT look at the story on the page below. Fill in the blanks on this page with the words called for. Then, using the words you have selected, fill in the blank spaces in the story.

Now you've created your own hilarious MAD LIBS® game!

THE GOOD SAMARITAN

VERB ENDING IN "ING" _____

NOUN _____

LAST NAME _____

NOUN _____

PART OF THE BODY (PLURAL) _____

VERB (PAST TENSE) _____

SAME LAST NAME _____

OCCUPATION _____

SOMETHING ALIVE (PLURAL) _____

A PLACE _____

NUMBER _____

TYPE OF FOOD _____

OCCUPATION _____

SAME LAST NAME _____

VERB ENDING IN "ING" _____

SAME LAST NAME _____

NOUN _____

MAD LIBS®

THE GOOD SAMARITAN

Today at school, I was _____ in the hallway, minding
                      VERB ENDING IN "ING"

my own _____, when I saw Bobby _____ coming
         NOUN   LAST NAME

out of _____ class. He had his _____ all
         NOUN   PART OF THE BODY (PLURAL)

scrunched up and looked mad. It turns out, he _____
                                               VERB (PAST TENSE)

his lunch money and no one would lend him any. This was probably

because _____ is the biggest _____ in the whole
         SAME LAST NAME   OCCUPATION

school! He's constantly teasing the other _____
                                           SOMETHING ALIVE (PLURAL)

and ends up in the principal's _____ at least _____
                               A PLACE   NUMBER

times a week. Later at lunch, I was really excited because today is

_____ Tuesday! I was just about to buy my tacos from the
TYPE OF FOOD

_____ behind the counter, when I saw _____
OCCUPATION   SAME LAST NAME

_____ at a table, alone. Then I thought of the story of
VERB ENDING IN "ING"

the Good Samaritan. So I gave him some of my lunch money. I was so

surprised when _____ smiled, probably for the first time
               SAME LAST NAME

ever in his whole _____!
                  NOUN

MAD LIBS® is fun to play with friends, but you can also play it by yourself! To begin with, DO NOT look at the story on the page below. Fill in the blanks on this page with the words called for. Then, using the words you have selected, fill in the blank spaces in the story.

Now you've created your own hilarious MAD LIBS® game!

SUNDAY MORNING COFFEE, JUICE, AND DOUGHNUTS

FIRST NAME _____

NUMBER _____

SOMETHING ALIVE (PLURAL) _____

TYPE OF LIQUID _____

ADJECTIVE _____

PLURAL NOUN _____

PLURAL NOUN _____

SILLY WORD _____

SAME SOMETHING ALIVE (PLURAL) _____

SAME TYPE OF LIQUID _____

PLURAL NOUN _____

PERSON YOU KNOW _____

TYPE OF FOOD _____

PERSON YOU KNOW _____

NUMBER _____

ARTICLE OF CLOTHING _____

PART OF THE BODY (PLURAL) _____

ADJECTIVE _____

MAD LIBS
SUNDAY MORNING COFFEE, JUICE, AND DOUGHNUTS

Mom says there's nothing like a good cup of _____ after
                                            FIRST NAME

church! Every Sunday morning at _____ o'clock, the youth
                                    NUMBER

group _____ are in charge of setting up for
        SOMETHING ALIVE (PLURAL)

coffee, orange _____, and doughnuts. The local coffee shop
                TYPE OF LIQUID

named _____ _____ donates _____
        ADJECTIVE   PLURAL NOUN   PLURAL NOUN

and lids. Most grown-ups sigh and say "_____" when they
                                          SILLY WORD

take a sip. The delicious coffee is just for the parents, not the kids or

_____. That's fine because doughnuts and
SAME SOMETHING ALIVE (PLURAL)

_____ are yummier, anyway! My favorite doughnut is
SAME TYPE OF LIQUID

the one with _____ on top, and _____ loves
              PLURAL NOUN   PERSON YOU KNOW

the glazed ones with the _____ filling. You're only supposed
                          TYPE OF FOOD

to take one doughnut, but we all know _____ stuffs
                                        PERSON YOU KNOW

_____ more in their _____. We all drive home
  NUMBER   ARTICLE OF CLOTHING

from church with our spirits lifted, our _____
                                          PART OF THE BODY (PLURAL)

sticky, and our bellies _____!
                          ADJECTIVE

MAD LIBS® is fun to play with friends, but you can also play it by yourself! To begin with, DO NOT look at the story on the page below. Fill in the blanks on this page with the words called for. Then, using the words you have selected, fill in the blank spaces in the story.

Now you've created your own hilarious MAD LIBS® game!

YOUTH GROUP LEADER QUIZ

ADJECTIVE _____

VEHICLE _____

TYPE OF LIQUID _____

NUMBER _____

TYPE OF FOOD _____

NOUN _____

TYPE OF FOOD (PLURAL) _____

NUMBER _____

PLURAL NOUN _____

PERSON YOU KNOW _____

PART OF THE BODY _____

EXCLAMATION _____

VERB _____

NOUN _____

PERSON YOU KNOW _____

NOUN _____

NUMBER _____

OCCUPATION _____

MAD LIBS®

YOUTH GROUP LEADER QUIZ

Would you make a good youth group leader? Take this _____
ADJECTIVE

quiz to find out!

1. Do you love God, and are you okay if the back seat of your

   _____ gets filled with empty _____ containers
   VEHICLE   TYPE OF LIQUID

   and starts to smell like _____-day-old _____?
                             NUMBER   TYPE OF FOOD

2. Are you ready to pull all-nighters where you go bowling, play laser

   _____, eat Canadian bacon and pineapple _____,
   NOUN   TYPE OF FOOD (PLURAL)

   and stick _____ plastic _____ into the front
              NUMBER   PLURAL NOUN

   lawn of _____?
            PERSON YOU KNOW

3. Do you find yourself smiling from _____-to-ear,
                                       PART OF THE BODY

   shouting " _____ " at the chance to _____ on
               EXCLAMATION   VERB

   Friday nights?

4. Do you love playing capture the _____ or singing worship
                                     NOUN

   songs while _____ plays the _____?
                PERSON YOU KNOW   NOUN

If you answered yes to these _____ questions, you might be the
                              NUMBER

perfect volunteer youth group _____!
                               OCCUPATION

MAD LIBS® is fun to play with friends, but you can also play it by yourself! To begin with, DO NOT look at the story on the page below. Fill in the blanks on this page with the words called for. Then, using the words you have selected, fill in the blank spaces in the story.

Now you've created your own hilarious MAD LIBS® game!

BEST BIBLE STUDY

FIRST NAME _____

SAME FIRST NAME _____

PLURAL NOUN _____

PLURAL NOUN _____

SILLY WORD _____

ADJECTIVE _____

VERB _____

PLURAL NOUN _____

A PLACE _____

TYPE OF BUILDING _____

NOUN _____

SOMETHING ALIVE (PLURAL) _____

VERB _____

VERB ENDING IN "S" _____

ADJECTIVE _____

MAD LIBS®

BEST BIBLE STUDY

I just had the best Bible study class ever! Pastor _____ really
FIRST NAME

knows how to make learning fun! We played Bible bingo, where Pastor

_____ reads stories from the Bible, and we have to match
SAME FIRST NAME

the stories to _____ on our bingo cards. The first one to get
PLURAL NOUN

five _____ in a row has to yell out "_____!" It's
PLURAL NOUN   SILLY WORD

so _____! I didn't _____ the game, but it was still
ADJECTIVE   VERB

fun to play with the other _____ in my class! Then we
PLURAL NOUN

played Bible tag outside in (the) _____. It was nice to get out
A PLACE

of the _____ and run around under the _____. In this game,
TYPE OF BUILDING   NOUN

one person is "it" and has to tag the other _____
SOMETHING ALIVE (PLURAL)

before they can recite a line from the Scripture! If they don't, then they

have to _____ "it" and the game _____ all over
VERB   VERB ENDING IN "S"

again. I'm not a very _____ runner, so I'm really glad I know
ADJECTIVE

my Scriptures!

MAD LIBS® is fun to play with friends, but you can also play it by yourself! To begin with, DO NOT look at the story on the page below. Fill in the blanks on this page with the words called for. Then, using the words you have selected, fill in the blank spaces in the story.

Now you've created your own hilarious MAD LIBS® game!

I'M GOING ON A MISSION TRIP

SOMETHING ALIVE (PLURAL) _____

ADVERB _____

A PLACE _____

NOUN _____

ADJECTIVE _____

NOUN _____

VEHICLE _____

PLURAL NOUN _____

NOUN _____

PLURAL NOUN _____

VERB _____

VERB ENDING IN "ING" _____

PART OF THE BODY (PLURAL) _____

NOUN _____

NOUN _____

VERB _____

YOUR NAME _____

MAD LIBS®
I'M GOING ON
A MISSION TRIP

Dear _____ and Family,
  SOMETHING ALIVE (PLURAL)

I'm _____ excited to announce that I'm going on a mission
  ADVERB

trip to (the) _____! During this trip, we will be building a/an
  A PLACE

_____ for a lovely and _____ family. Prior to arrival,
  NOUN   ADJECTIVE

the house's _____ will be poured and the lumber will be
  NOUN

delivered in a/an _____. To construct a wall, we'll hammer
  VEHICLE

lots of _____ into the wood to join the pieces. The family
  PLURAL NOUN

will help, too, and together we'll install the electrical _____
  NOUN

and the bathroom _____. During lunch, we'll use a soccer
  PLURAL NOUN

ball to _____ with the children. It's a great time to connect
  VERB

and form _____ bonds with a wonderful family. We'd
  VERB ENDING IN "ING"

love your help! First, pray! There's nothing like good wishes to fill our

_____ with joy. You can also make a/an
  PART OF THE BODY (PLURAL)

_____ to help with the costs. All donations are _____-deductible.
  NOUN   NOUN

Thank you for partnering with us to _____ a better world!
  VERB

Loving His people,

_____
  YOUR NAME

MAD LIBS® is fun to play with friends, but you can also play it by yourself! To begin with, DO NOT look at the story on the page below. Fill in the blanks on this page with the words called for. Then, using the words you have selected, fill in the blank spaces in the story.

Now you've created your own hilarious MAD LIBS® game!

SINGING IN THE CHOIR

ADJECTIVE _____

NOUN _____

NUMBER _____

OCCUPATION (PLURAL) _____

VERB _____

PLURAL NOUN _____

NOUN _____

ADJECTIVE _____

PLURAL NOUN _____

TYPE OF EVENT _____

NUMBER _____

EXCLAMATION _____

VERB _____

ARTICLE OF CLOTHING _____

ADVERB _____

VERB _____

CELEBRITY _____

MAD LIBS®

SINGING IN THE CHOIR

Today, my _____ friends and I had rehearsal for the church
                ADJECTIVE

choir. Our singing teacher, Ms. Mc-_____, separated everyone
                                    NOUN

in the choir into _____ groups, by whether they were altos,
                    NUMBER

sopranos, or _____. Then we learned how to _____
              OCCUPATION (PLURAL)   VERB

sheet music. There were lots of different _____ on the
                                            PLURAL NOUN

pages. We had to learn the difference between a half _____
                                                      NOUN

and a/an _____ note. Then we all sang "Jingle _____"
          ADJECTIVE   PLURAL NOUN

to prepare for the Christmas _____, which is coming up in
                              TYPE OF EVENT

just _____ weeks. _____! I can't believe we have to
      NUMBER   EXCLAMATION

_____ in front of over two hundred people. I don't even have
 VERB

my choir _____ yet! My mom says I'll sing
          ARTICLE OF CLOTHING

_____ as long as I remember to practice, practice, and then
 ADVERB

_____ some more! But I think it's going to take a lot more
 VERB

than practice for me to sing like _____! So I'll make sure to
                                   CELEBRITY

say a special prayer to God the night before the concert, just to be safe.

From KEEP THE FAITH MAD LIBS® • Copyright © 2023 by Penguin Random House LLC

MAD LIBS® is fun to play with friends, but you can also play it by yourself! To begin with, DO NOT look at the story on the page below. Fill in the blanks on this page with the words called for. Then, using the words you have selected, fill in the blank spaces in the story.

Now you've created your own hilarious MAD LIBS® game!

FAMILY CAMP

NOUN _____

PLURAL NOUN _____

NOUN _____

ADJECTIVE _____

TYPE OF FOOD _____

NOUN _____

PLURAL NOUN _____

VERB _____

ADJECTIVE _____

YOUR NAME _____

VERB _____

A PLACE _____

NOUN _____

TYPE OF FOOD (PLURAL) _____

ADJECTIVE _____

PLURAL NOUN _____

PART OF THE BODY (PLURAL) _____

VERB ENDING IN "ING" _____

Family camp is my favorite part of summer! Every church family brings

their own _____ to sleep in. Don't forget to secure your tent
      NOUN

by hammering the long _____ into the _____.
                      PLURAL NOUN   NOUN

Every day we compete in _____ competitions, like _____
                         ADJECTIVE   TYPE OF FOOD

toss, _____-ball, and musical _____. For our
      NOUN   PLURAL NOUN

limbo contest, we _____ under a hiking stick and play the
                   VERB

song "Don't Worry, Be _____." Pastor _____'s
                       ADJECTIVE   YOUR NAME

favorite competition is the one where you _____ across the
                                           VERB

grassy _____ in your sleeping bag. At night, we sit around a
        A PLACE

roaring _____ and roast _____ while singing
         NOUN   TYPE OF FOOD (PLURAL)

_____ songs. Once we're tucked into our sleeping bags,
 ADJECTIVE

sometimes we shine our flashlights and create shadow _____
                                                      PLURAL NOUN

with our _____. I can't wait! I'm going to start
          PART OF THE BODY (PLURAL)

_____ my backpack tomorrow!
 VERB ENDING IN "ING"

MAD LIBS® is fun to play with friends, but you can also play it by yourself! To begin with, DO NOT look at the story on the page below. Fill in the blanks on this page with the words called for. Then, using the words you have selected, fill in the blank spaces in the story.

Now you've created your own hilarious MAD LIBS® game!

THE RULES FOR CAPTURE THE FLAG

VERB _____

VERB _____

A PLACE _____

SOMETHING ALIVE (PLURAL) _____

PERSON YOU KNOW _____

CELEBRITY _____

VERB _____

YOUR NAME _____

CELEBRITY _____

NOUN _____

SILLY WORD _____

A PLACE _____

VERB ENDING IN "ING" _____

SOMETHING ALIVE _____

VERB ENDING IN "ING" _____

NOUN _____

ADVERB _____

A PLACE _____

MAD LIBS®
THE RULES FOR
CAPTURE THE FLAG

Here's how to play _____ the flag:
_{VERB}

1. The goal of the game is for each team to _____ the other
   _{VERB}

   team's flag and take it back to its _____ .
   _{A PLACE}

2. Pick positions for all the _____ on your
   _{SOMETHING ALIVE (PLURAL)}

   team. _____ and _____ should try to
   _{PERSON YOU KNOW}   _{CELEBRITY}

   _____ the other team's flag. _____ and others
   _{VERB}   _{YOUR NAME}

   like _____ should guard your own _____ and
   _{CELEBRITY}   _{NOUN}

   scare the opponent by shouting _____!
   _{SILLY WORD}

3. If members of the other team enter your team's _____,
   _{A PLACE}

   you can send them to "jail" by _____ them. Players
   _{VERB ENDING IN "ING"}

   can be freed from jail when a fellow _____ touches them.
   _{SOMETHING ALIVE}

4. A team wins by _____ the other team's _____
   _{VERB ENDING IN "ING"}   _{NOUN}

   and taking it _____ to their own _____.
   _{ADVERB}   _{A PLACE}

MAD LIBS® is fun to play with friends, but you can also play it by yourself! To begin with, DO NOT look at the story on the page below. Fill in the blanks on this page with the words called for. Then, using the words you have selected, fill in the blank spaces in the story.

Now you've created your own hilarious MAD LIBS® game!

CHURCH BAND REHEARSAL

YOUR NAME _____

NOUN _____

PERSON YOU KNOW _____

EXCLAMATION _____

CELEBRITY _____

NUMBER _____

PART OF THE BODY _____

SAME CELEBRITY _____

SILLY WORD _____

A SOUND _____

SOMETHING ALIVE _____

SAME PERSON YOU KNOW _____

ANIMAL _____

A PLACE _____

YOUR NAME _____

ADJECTIVE _____

MAD LIBS®

CHURCH BAND REHEARSAL

_____: Let's start with a really uplifting song, like "I Could
YOUR NAME

Sing of Your _____ Forever."
NOUN

_____: _____! After the intro, _____,
PERSON YOU KNOW   EXCLAMATION   CELEBRITY

can you come in with the bongos? Use one, two, or _____
NUMBER

fingers rather than your whole _____.
PART OF THE BODY

_____: Great idea! I'll add background vocals by singing
SAME CELEBRITY

"_____" and making _____ noises. Can we close with
SILLY WORD   A SOUND

"Amazing Grace"? I can sing that like a/an _____.
SOMETHING ALIVE

_____: And I can hit the high notes like a/an
SAME PERSON YOU KNOW

_____ from (the) _____!
ANIMAL   A PLACE

_____: Let's do it! Sunday is going to be _____!
YOUR NAME   ADJECTIVE

God will be smiling from heaven!

From KEEP THE FAITH MAD LIBS® • Copyright © 2023 by Penguin Random House LLC

MAD LIBS® is fun to play with friends, but you can also play it by yourself! To begin with, DO NOT look at the story on the page below. Fill in the blanks on this page with the words called for. Then, using the words you have selected, fill in the blank spaces in the story.

Now you've created your own hilarious MAD LIBS® game!

WHAT BIBLE CHARACTER AM I?

ADJECTIVE _____

VERB _____

ANIMAL (PLURAL) _____

ANIMAL (PLURAL) _____

SOMETHING ALIVE (PLURAL) _____

ANIMAL _____

TYPE OF FOOD _____

ADJECTIVE _____

ADJECTIVE _____

ADVERB _____

VERB _____

PLURAL NOUN _____

ADJECTIVE _____

PLURAL NOUN _____

VERB (PAST TENSE) _____

NOUN _____

Guess the names of these biblical characters:

• I was swallowed by a/an _____ fish. The fish _____
   ADJECTIVE   VERB

me back onto land.

• I built a boat and invited two of every animal: _____,
                          ANIMAL (PLURAL)

_____, and even _____.
ANIMAL (PLURAL)   SOMETHING ALIVE (PLURAL)

• I baptized Jesus, and I wore clothing made of _____ hair
                               ANIMAL

and ate locusts and _____ made by bumblebees.
              TYPE OF FOOD

• I was almost fed to _____ lions because I prayed to God.
             ADJECTIVE

• My strength lay in my _____ hair until Delilah
                 ADJECTIVE

_____ decided to _____ it.
ADVERB   VERB

• I'm a king who asked God for wisdom. As a result, I knew everything

about _____ and _____ _____.
    PLURAL NOUN   ADJECTIVE   PLURAL NOUN

• I _____ a giant with just a slingshot and a/an
   VERB (PAST TENSE)

_____.
NOUN

Answers: Jonah, Noah, John the Baptist, Daniel, Samson, Solomon,

David

MAD LIBS® is fun to play with friends, but you can also play it by yourself! To begin with, DO NOT look at the story on the page below. Fill in the blanks on this page with the words called for. Then, using the words you have selected, fill in the blank spaces in the story.

Now you've created your own hilarious MAD LIBS® game!

MY SCHOOL'S NATIVITY PLAY

A PLACE _____

SOMETHING ALIVE (PLURAL) _____

TYPE OF BUILDING _____

VERB _____

PLURAL NOUN _____

NUMBER _____

ANIMAL (PLURAL) _____

SILLY WORD _____

FIRST NAME _____

NOUN _____

TYPE OF CONTAINER (PLURAL) _____

PLURAL NOUN _____

PLURAL NOUN _____

NOUN _____

COLOR _____

ADJECTIVE _____

VERB _____

PLURAL NOUN _____

Each Christmas, our church puts on a Christmas pageant in (the)

_____. All the _____ in our middle
A PLACE   SOMETHING ALIVE (PLURAL)

_____ are allowed to _____ in the play. The older
TYPE OF BUILDING   VERB

_____ usually get to play Mary and Joseph or one of the
PLURAL NOUN

_____ Wise Men, while the younger kids get to dress up as
NUMBER

_____. The sheep don't have any lines and only have to
ANIMAL (PLURAL)

say "_____" once in a while. Since we don't have any real
SILLY WORD

gold, _____-incense, and _____ for the Wise Men to
FIRST NAME   NOUN

give to the baby Jesus, we use fancy perfume _____
TYPE OF CONTAINER (PLURAL)

instead. The manger is made of old cardboard _____
PLURAL NOUN

painted to look like wooden _____. To make the _____
PLURAL NOUN   NOUN

that guided the Wise Men to Jesus, we use some _____ paint
COLOR

and lots and lots of _____ glitter! Even the hay isn't real. It's
ADJECTIVE

made of paper we _____ into strips using safety _____.
VERB   PLURAL NOUN

But one thing is very real in our play: our love for Jesus!

Join the millions of Mad Libs fans
creating wacky and wonderful
stories on our apps!

Download **Mad Libs** today!